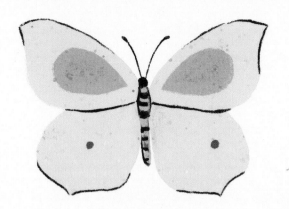

Cleopatra
Gonepteryx cleopatra

Blue Pansy
Precis orythia

Hercules Beetle
Dynastes hercules

Chalkhill Blue
Polyommatus coridon

Fiery Acraea
Acraea acrita

2-Spot Lady Beetle
Adalia bipunctata

Honey Bee
Apis mellifera

Madagascar Giant Swallowtail
Pharmacophagus antenor

15-Spot Lady Beetle
Anatis 15-punctata

Forest Mother-of-Pearl
Salamis parhassus

SPECIMEN No.

This book belongs to:

T0026683

Name _____

Darwin very much enjoyed observing and collecting insects.
Test your skills at being a naturalist by using the insect chart
on the end pages to find and identify some of the
beetle and butterfly species inside the book.

The Darwin family illustration in this edition has been updated
to include Darwin's two children who died in infancy.

Visit us on the Web! rhcbooks.com

Educators and librarians, for a variety of teaching tools,
visit us at RHTeachersLibrarians.com

Library of Congress Cataloging-in-Publication Data
Names: Radeva, Sabina (Graphic artist), author.
Title: Charles Darwin's On the Origin of Species / adapted and illustrated by Sabina Radeva.
Other titles: On the Origin of Species
Description: New York: Crown Books for Young Readers, [2019] | Audience: Age 4–8. | Audience: K to grade 3.
Identifiers: LCCN 2018057034 | ISBN 978-1-9848-9491-5 (hc) | ISBN 978-1-9848-9492-2 (glb) | ISBN 978-1-9848-9493-9 (epub)
Subjects: LCSH: Darwin, Charles, 1809–1882. On the origin of species. |
Evolution (Biology)—Juvenile literature. | Natural selection—Juvenile literature.
Classification: LCC QH367.1 .R245 2019 | DDC 576.8/2—dc23

The text of this book is set in 12-point Futura.
Interior design by Elizabeth Tardiff

MANUFACTURED IN CHINA
10 9 8 7 6 5 4 3 2 1
First American Edition

CHARLES DARWIN'S

On the
ORIGIN
of
SPECIES

Adapted and Illustrated
by Sabina Radeva

Crown Books for Young Readers

New York

A long, long time ago, before humans even existed, the living world looked very different from how it looks today. Since life on Earth began, tiny organisms, plants and animals have been changing slowly, over millions of years, because of a process we call evolution.

For most of human history, many people believed that everything in the world was created all at once. They thought that plants, animals and people were always the same as they are now.

But there were a few clever and curious scientists who challenged this idea.

Animals change over time, and they often look different in different parts of the world.

Georges-Louis Leclerc de Buffon

Ancestor with short neck

Huh?

Hmm, perhaps giraffes who give their necks a good stretch to reach the higher leaves will go on to have baby giraffes with extra-stretched necks?

Jean-Baptiste Lamarck

French biologist Jean-Baptiste Lamarck liked the idea that some animals evolved by using certain body parts more than others. It turned out he was a little off the mark with that theory, but it certainly did get people thinking!

✳ See Appendix VI

Scientists were right to notice that living things changed – or evolved – over time, but nobody was quite sure *how* this happened.

Soon, though, the world came to know Charles Darwin, an English naturalist who would change people's understanding of how different species came to be.

Darwin traveled the globe on board the HMS *Beagle*,
visiting wondrous lands, studying animals and collecting fossils.
Many things excited and amazed him on his adventures,
and he wrote them all down as accurately as he could.

Rhea darwinii

HMS Beagle

Fossils

Down House

The Darwin Family

Charles Robert Darwin

Emma Wedgwood

William Erasmus

Anne Elizabeth

Henrietta Emma

George Howard

Elizabeth

Francis

Leonard

Horace

Charles Waring

Polly

Mary Eleanor

When Darwin returned from his expedition, he worked from his English country house, where he lived with his wife, children, and his dog Polly!

But Darwin had another long and difficult journey ahead. He had a new, big idea he wanted to share with everyone, but to explain it, he would have to do a lot of writing, studying and discussing with other scientists.

Who is studying who here?

Darwin liked to study the orangutan Jenny at the London Zoo.

The greenhouse was one of Darwin's favorite spots. He conducted many intriguing experiments there.

ON THE ORIGIN OF SPECIES

✳ See Appendix I

In 1859, after twenty years of hard work, Darwin was finally able to publish his book, *On the Origin of Species*, which explained all of his ideas.

In his book, Darwin explains that **species** are groups of living things that look alike and can have babies together. But even if they belong to the same species, no two animals are *exactly* the same.

Look closer and you will see some are:

TALLER

SHORTER

"*I look at the term species, as one arbitrarily given for the sake of convenience to a set of individuals closely resembling each other.*"

FASTER

SLOWER

or different in
COLOR!

These differences are known as variations.

Variation Under Domestication

Poodle

Bloodhound

Pug

English pointer

Italian greyhound

Bulldog

Animals that people have tamed and domesticated, like pets and farm animals, look very different from their wild ancestors. Take man's best friend, for example – we now have over 340 dog breeds! People have raised them for their different sizes, shapes, colors and even talents. Yet all of these breeds came from one kind of wild wolf, many howling moons ago!

"Great as the differences are between the breeds of pigeons, I am fully convinced that the common opinion of naturalists is correct, namely, that all have descended from the rock pigeon."

Columba livia, or Rock pigeon

Fantail

English pouter

Short-faced tumbler

English carrier

Scandaroon

English barb

Trumpeter

Jacobin

Frillback

Darwin studied pigeons too. Just like dogs, Darwin knew that all pigeons belong to the same species, although you certainly wouldn't think so by looking at them!

Gardeners may encourage the growth of plants with large and beautiful flowers while they might weed out those that don't quite make the grade.

Like pets, farm animals and even garden flowers can look very different from their wild ancestors. This is mostly because people make choices. Farmers may choose to breed the cows that produce the most milk, the chickens that lay the best eggs, and the sheep with the warmest and most knittable wool.

Variation Under Nature

Species change in the wild too. Even without human influence of any kind, plants sprout and young animals in the wild are born, all with slight differences. Some differences don't matter, some are not helpful at all . . .

. . . but some differences are very useful.

Darwin noted that Galápagos finches have developed beaks in all sorts of shapes and sizes. These differences help them to pick up their favorite snacks. Different beaks are good for different nibbles.

Large beak for crushing tough seeds

Small beak for feeding on soft seeds

Pointed beak that can hold tools to probe and find insects

Long and sharp beak helps to tear cactus flowers

Struggle for Existence

Nature may be beautiful and abundant, but living
in the wilderness is not easy for any species.
Many can't escape their predators or
find the right conditions to survive.

"Every organic being naturally increases at so high a rate, that, if not destroyed, the earth would soon be covered by the progeny of a single pair."

Animals compete for food and shelter – things they must have if they are to survive and have babies. It's a struggle to live in the wild, and only the best adapted will succeed.

"*I estimated that the winter of 1854-55 destroyed four-fifths of the birds in my own grounds.*"

"We see beautiful adaptations everywhere and in every part of the organic world."

Natural Selection

Some differences help animals survive in the wild. Some help them to hide, to hunt, to live longer or have lots of babies. Those babies will then grow to benefit from the helpful differences that have been passed down from their parents. The species is adapting to the world around it.

"A grain in the balance will determine which individual shall live and which shall die - which variety or species shall increase in number, and which shall decrease, or finally become extinct."

Even small differences in color or design can help an animal or plant to live, survive and reproduce better. Darwin called this **Natural Selection**.

Pink-downed peach

Yellow smooth peach

The Curculio beetle loves to feed on yellow smooth peaches.
Trees with pink-downed peaches are pestered less often by
this beetle, so they reproduce better and increase in number.

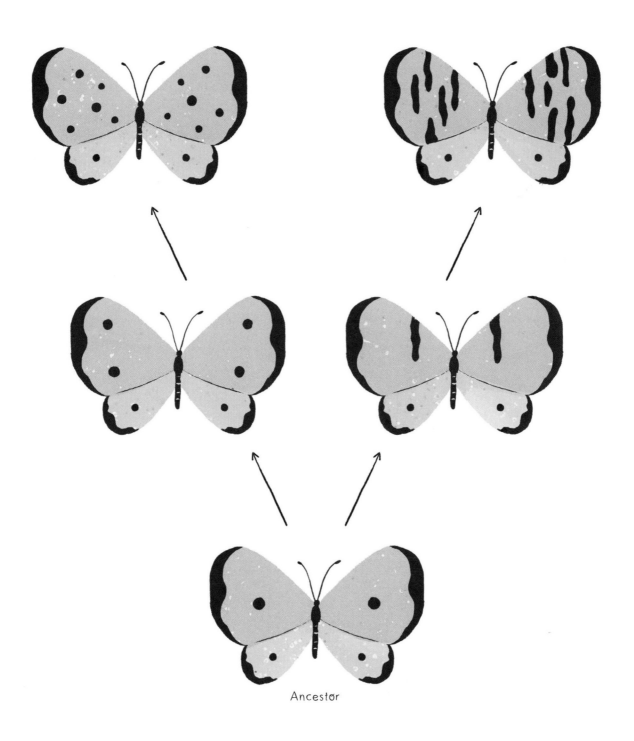

Ancestor

Over a really long time, these little differences can add up and a species can change so much that they become a whole new species. Darwin suggested that this is a really slow process, taking tens of thousands of years. That's why it's hard to see evolution happening with our own eyes.

Of course, just as new species form, others die out or become extinct.

✳ See Appendixes IV and V

Horse

Zebra

Donkey

Closely related plants and animals
all come from one original species.
The wider group of relatives
is called a genus.

Sometimes features that seem to have
vanished forever can suddenly reappear.
For example, some Devonshire ponies
are born with stripes just like zebras,
which suggests they may share
a stripy common ancestor!

"As buds give rise by growth to fresh buds, and these, if vigorous, branch out and overtop on all sides many a feebler branch, so by generation I believe it has been with the great Tree of Life, which fills with its dead and broken branches the crust of the earth, and covers the surface with its ever branching and beautiful ramifications."

Darwin drew a picture of a tree to show how species evolve. Scientists have taken this idea even further and shown that humans, animals, plants, insects and even the tiniest creatures are all descended from the first living things that ever came to be.

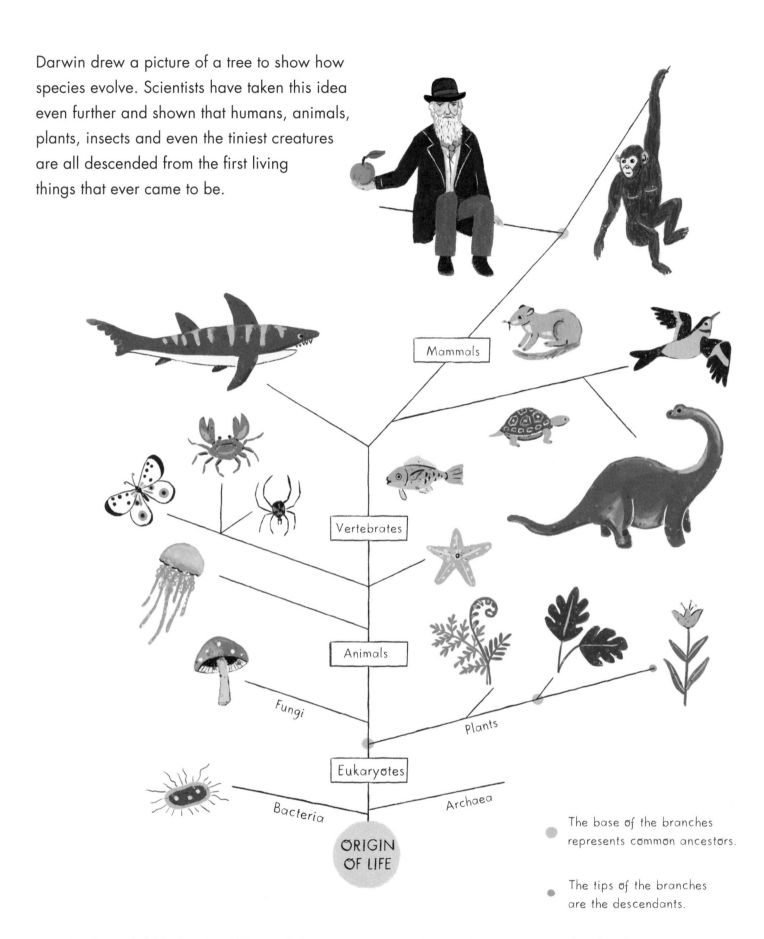

Mammals

Vertebrates

Animals

Fungi

Plants

Eukaryotes

Bacteria

Archaea

ORIGIN OF LIFE

The base of the branches represents common ancestors.

The tips of the branches are the descendants.

So how did life begin? Where did it first come from? Darwin wasn't sure, but his theory explains how it evolved into the many living things we see on planet Earth today.

"Why, if species have descended from other species by insensibly fine gradations, do we not everywhere see innumerable transitional forms? Why is not all nature in confusion, instead of the species being, as we see them, well defined?"

Difficulties on Theory

Darwin knew that his theory was difficult to prove,
and that people would ask questions about it.
His book is filled with answers to those questions –
for example: if species gradually change over time,
why do we not see many in-between forms, in the
middle of all these changes?

Darwin explained that Natural Selection makes living things better adapted to where
they live. Once animals with more useful traits appear, they will compete and replace
those that are less adapted.

"The crust of the earth is a vast museum."

Fossils are evidence of extinct species – like dinosaurs, woolly mammoths and the dodo bird – but there weren't many fossils to show species as they were changing. Darwin explained that this is because perfect conditions are needed for fossils to form, and those conditions are pretty rare.

Imperfections of the Geological Record

As rocks get bashed by the wind and sea, they break down into pieces called sediment.

Sediment

When animals die and get covered in layers of sediment, like a blanket, they can be preserved in sedimentary rocks.

Soft sediment

Compact

But the chances of this happening are very small, so we'll never know just how weird and wonderful many extinct species might have been!

"Can we believe that natural selection could produce, on the one hand, organs of trifling importance, such as the tail of a giraffe, which serves as a fly-flapper, and, on the other hand, organs of such wonderful structure, as the eye, of which we hardly as yet fully understand the inimitable perfection?"

Organs of Extreme Perfection

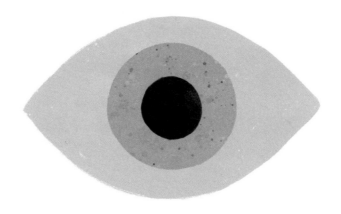

EVOLUTION OF THE EYE

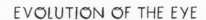

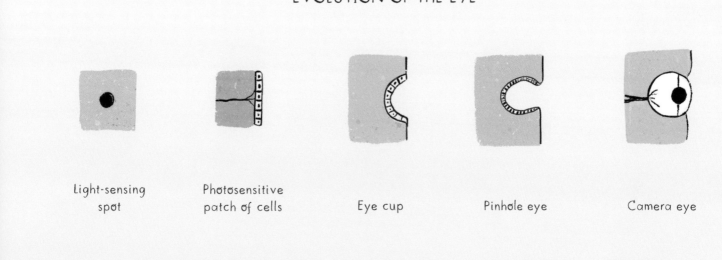

| Light-sensing spot | Photosensitive patch of cells | Eye cup | Pinhole eye | Camera eye |

According to Darwin, animals become more complicated as they evolve and new body parts are made from the old designs, rather than being started from scratch. Very complex organs like eyes evolved from what were simple designs to begin with. The eye was formed by tiny changes and upgrades over millions of years.

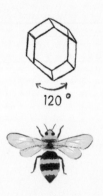

120°

"What shall we say to so marvelous an instinct as that which leads the bee to make cells, which have practically anticipated the discoveries of profound mathematicians?"

Instinct

Natural Selection doesn't just focus on how creatures look, but also on how they behave. Instinct is the seemingly magical way an animal is born knowing how to work with its environment. For example, many birds somehow know they must travel to warmer places during winter, and honey bees create perfect hexagon shapes in which to store their honey without ever being taught. These are examples of instincts, and if an instinct helps an animal to survive better, it can be kept and passed on to future generations.

Mountains, rivers and seas create natural barriers to migration, and many animals have difficulty crossing oceans.

Plant seeds can be carried or eaten by birds and "deposited" later, allowing them to spread more easily. This is why plants around the world often seem similar, but animals in different places are more different!

MIGRATION

MIGRATION

Ancestor species

Darwin explained how species spread around the world by something called migration. New species that start in one place will sometimes move to other places. In their new environment, the species will often change even more.

Migration

Because islands are surrounded by water and cut off from the mainland, they have become home to some of the most unusual animals on the planet. One BIG example of these unusual animals, spotted by Darwin, was a giant tortoise in the Galápagos Islands.

Pinta

GALÁPAGOS ISLANDS

Isabela

Floreana

Española

550 pounds (250kg)

It is thought that an ancestor of that tortoise floated to the island. With no predators or other large plant-eaters to compete with for food, the tortoise did very well for herself, as did her descendants. So far, evolution has caused the giant tortoise to get bigger and bigger over time, and it now weighs in at over 550 pounds.

Dolphins evolved from mammal ancestors.

Sharks evolved from fish ancestors.

Ichthyosaurs had reptile ancestors.

Interestingly, some animals have developed similar body parts without being closely related, just by living in the same environment.

Mutual Affinities of Organic Beings

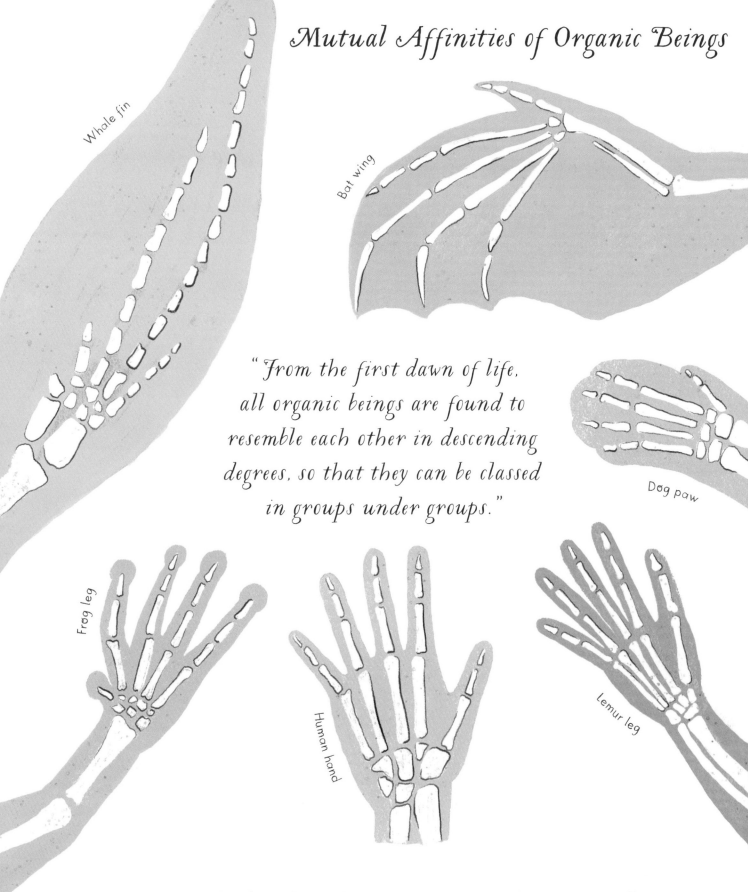

Whale fin

Bat wing

Dog paw

Frog leg

Human hand

Lemur leg

"From the first dawn of life, all organic beings are found to resemble each other in descending degrees, so that they can be classed in groups under groups."

Naturalists usually rely on the insides and bones to find out if species are really related. For example, many species share the same five-fingered bone structure in their hands, paws or flippers. This points to a shared branch in the tree of evolution.

CHICKEN EMBRYO   HUMAN EMBRYO

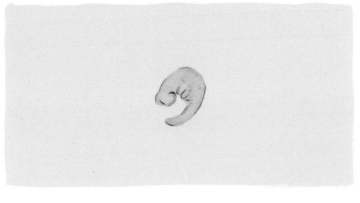

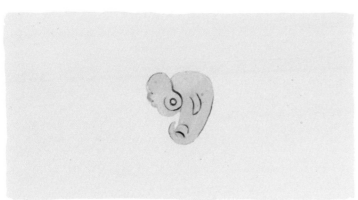

Before any animal is born or hatched, it is a tiny being called an embryo. At the very first stages, some embryos are quite difficult to tell apart. These similarities show that all animals are related at some level. Each creature has evolved its own different features based on the same basic blueprint for a creature's beginnings here on Earth.

❋ See Appendix VIII

Indohyus

Pakicetus

Ambulocetus natans

Dorudon

Rudimentary
hind leg bones

Many animals have bones, organs and other parts that don't have a purpose, but were very important for their ancestors. Because they don't harm the animal's chance of survival, these leftovers haven't disappeared even though they're no longer of any use. From the remains of our own lost tails to the leftover leg bones from a whale's time walking on the land, our bodies tell the history of our evolution.

"In the distant future I see open fields for far more important researches ... Light will be thrown on the origin of man and his history."

" Whilst this planet has gone cycling on according to the fixed law of gravity, from so simple a beginning endless forms most beautiful and most wonderful have been and are being evolved."

Conclusion

Darwin's Theory of Evolution by Natural Selection:

1.

All living things are born with slight variations or differences.

2.

Some differences help with survival and having babies, and
are passed down through generations.

3.

Many species have lots of babies, some of which will not survive.

4.

Those that survive are better adapted to living and breeding
in that environment.

5.

Useful traits that can be passed down through generations
will become more common in the population,
eventually leading to evolution.

Darwin's book comes to an end, but the process of evolution keeps going. For as
long as the cycle of life goes on, we will adapt and evolve alongside our fellow
animals and plants here on planet Earth.

Author's Note

Dear reader, I have attempted here to create a faithful picture-book adaptation of *On the Origin of Species* by Charles Darwin. From this book children can learn the power of observation and recognize how curiosity about the natural world can lead to incredible discoveries. Even without modern technology, Darwin was able to conduct enough credible research to transform our understanding of life on Earth.

There was a lot of fascinating information to cover, so I wasn't able to include much of his journey on HMS *Beagle*. For those fans who are eager to see more of the journey depicted, I have recommended some excellent picture books that can complete your Darwin collection.

You will notice that I have omitted some information from Darwin's original text because the concepts were too difficult for young readers. In consultation with many respected and accredited scientific collaborators, we agreed to leave out certain chapters and change the order of information to enhance the clarity of the work. It was difficult to adapt the content from a very dense and scientific book to be appropriate for the picture-book age level; however, I researched early-learning resources about evolution to make sure the necessary information was included.

With our ever-increasing knowledge, it became clear that certain aspects of the original text are outdated. Where this is the case, I have stayed true to Darwin's original findings in the main text, while adding the most notable scientific discoveries in the Appendix. It is also worth noting that when compiling *On the Origin of Species*, Darwin carefully avoided any speculation on the human origin, probably to avoid even further controversy at the time. Later he dedicated *The Descent of Man* to this topic.

Appendix

I. **Alfred Russel Wallace** was another British scientist who developed a theory similar to Darwin's. This encouraged Darwin to finally finish his book. Their work was published together in one paper in 1858. Darwin spent longer developing his theory, and as a respected naturalist he became known as the father of the evolutionary theory.

Alfred Russel Wallace

II. DNA and Genes

All living things are made of tiny units called cells. Most cells contain a code carried on a molecule called DNA. It looks like a spiraling ladder, a shape known as a double helix. Within each string of DNA are sets of instructions. The genetic code carries all the information that decides what a living thing will grow up to be like.

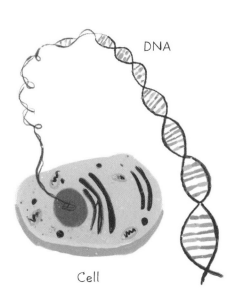

DNA

Cell

III. Inheritance

To inherit something means it has been passed down to you from your parents, grandparents, great-grandparents and so on. Inheritance in genetic terms is the way a living thing looks or behaves, and how that is passed down through generations. Our unique design is determined by the genes we inherit from our parents.

Parent

Children

IV. Variation and Mutations

Darwin still didn't quite know everything about inheritance or how variations occur in order to be passed to the next generation. Now we know that DNA drives evolution. Sudden changes in genes are called mutations. Sometimes mutations alter the way a living thing looks or functions, and such mutations are the reason variations exist.

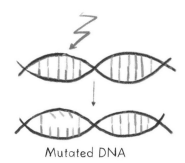

Mutated DNA

Steppe mammoth   Cold environment   Woolly mammoth

V. Natural Selection

Darwin thought evolution by Natural Selection was gradual and ongoing. However, every so often, a new mutation has had a big impact and allowed species to evolve very quickly. Major environmental changes, such as ice ages, have also sped up evolution, as animals race to adapt to new challenges.

Starving parent

Babies may store more fat to survive harsh conditions.

VI. Epigenetics

Scientists have found that lifestyles and habits can affect the expression of genes without directly changing their code. These effects can also be passed to offspring. A starving animal may produce babies who store more fat from their food, for example. We still don't completely understand the mechanisms of epigenetics, but we know Jean-Baptiste Lamarck was not completely wrong about his theory that changes based on an animal's lifestyle can be passed down to new generations.

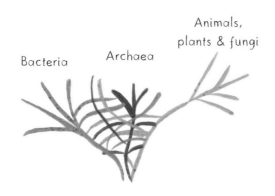

Bacteria   Archaea   Animals, plants & fungi

VII. The Tangled Thicket of Life

Darwin sketched a tree-like picture to explain the origins and relationships of species. However, new findings show that occasionally DNA can move between branches from species to species, through viruses carrying DNA, for instance. This has led many scientists to insist that the Tree of Life should look more like a tangled shrub.

VIII. Comparative Embryology

In early years, scientists like Ernst Haeckel wrongly proposed that all embryos repeat stages of evolution and all embryos look identical at the very first stages of development. This theory was disproved. Nowadays modern science shows that species that have similar embryonic development are closely related and probably have a common ancestor.

Misconceptions

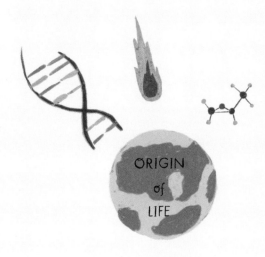

Evolution explains the origin of life on Earth.

No, this is a misconception (a mistaken belief). The theory of evolution does not explain how life on Earth started. Darwin's theory explains how species can change over time, and how new species are created from existing species, by the process of Natural Selection.

Evolution proves that we evolved from monkeys.

No, humans did not evolve from monkeys as we know them now. All primates shared a common ancestor some 25 to 30 million years ago, and both monkeys and humans evolved from this animal in lots of different ways, until we became the species we are today. Modern primates, like monkeys and apes, are more like cousins. You are descended from your parents, but you are only *related* to your cousins.

Evolution is when one kind of animal gives birth to another kind of animal.

No, an individual animal can never give birth to a completely new kind, or species, of animal. For example, a cat will never give birth to a dog. Instead, young animals are born with small differences, and after many generations the species gradually changes.

You can't see evolution happening.

Evolution is a very slow process that takes thousands of years. In a human lifetime, we can see only a snapshot of the creation of a new species. However, in the laboratory, scientists have been able to see how bacteria, plants and fruit flies mutate and change. In the wild, many insects have built up a resistance to pesticides. When we see these changes, we are observing evolution.

Human lifetime

Glossary

Adapt
To modify or adjust to new conditions or a new environment

Adaptation
A special feature or way of behaving that helps a living thing to survive

Ancestor
An earlier form of an animal or plant from which the others have evolved

Descendant
A living thing that has descended from a particular ancestor

DNA
The substance that carries genetic information within the cells of all living things

Evolve
To change or develop very gradually over time

Extinct
Species no longer in existence, without any living members

Fossil
The ancient remains of an animal or plant preserved in layers of rock

Generation
A group of plants or animals born and living in the same period of time

Genes
Small sections of DNA, which together determine the characteristics of a living thing

Genus
A group of related species of plants or animals

Naturalist
A person or scientist who studies and appreciates nature

Offspring
The children or young of a specific parent or parents

Primates
A large and diverse group of mammals, including humans, apes and monkeys

Sediment
Small pieces of rocks/soil that sink and settle in layers

Species
A group of animals or plants that are similar and can produce offspring together

Variation
A different version of something, distinct from similar life-forms

Dedication and Credits

Kickstarter: This book would not exist without the support of my Kickstarter backers. I am very grateful to all of you! Special thanks to Shelbie Bartlett, Schuyler Huff, Pierre-François Cohadon and Louise Hargis for providing feedback on my work in progress. Also thanks to Holly Schineller, Paul Tinkler, Sean Rainey, Craig Kovach and Erica Behr.

Story advice: I am especially grateful to the talented and amazing children's writer Tamara Forge, who consulted and edited my text. Jade LaRue West further helped to bring it into shape. A special thanks to my agent Veronique Baxter.

Science help: Big thanks to Claire Asher, who reviewed the book content and advised me on the scientific accuracy. Thanks also to Nigel Borg and Lia Stelea.

Editing: I want to thank my fantastic editor, Anna Barnes, from Penguin Random House, whose enthusiasm for this project resulted in the book being picked up for publishing! Thanks to Emily Lunn for proofing my text and spreads. Thank you to Emily Easton, Samantha Gentry and the entire team at Random House Children's Books for embracing my book across the pond.

Layout and design: Many thanks to Keren Greenfeld and Katherine Lodge, who worked hard and ensured the perfect look of the book.

Further help and support: Thank you to the wider team at Penguin Random House. Thanks to the University of Hertfordshire and my tutors Barbara Brownie, Thomas Cuschieri and Kate Milner for supervising my work and for encouraging me. My friend, picture book illustrator Denise Holmes, for mentoring me and teaching me all about picture books. Thanks to Lizzy Doyle for inspiring me. To @_CROPES_ on Twitter for his brilliant Common Creationist Misconceptions, which provided insight on misconceptions about evolution. Thanks to English Heritage for allowing me to sketch at the site of Darwin's house. My husband, Alexander, who reviewed my text and helped with the kids when I needed some time to escape and work. I am grateful to my daughter Sophia for her honest feedback on my illustrations and text, and to my parents for cheering me and supporting me.

Recommended Reading

There are some wonderfully informative books on the topic of evolution that you might enjoy for further reading.

Charles Darwin's Around the World Adventure by Jennifer Thermes

Grandmother Fish by Jonathan Tweet and Karen Lewis

The Mystery of Darwin's Frog by Marty Crump, Steve Jenkins, and Edel Rodriguez

Our Family Tree: An Evolution Story by Lisa Westberg Peters and Lauren Stringer

The Tree of Life by Peter Sís

What Darwin Saw: The Journey That Changed the World by Rosalyn Schanzer

Who Was Charles Darwin? by Deborah Hopkinson and Nancy Harrison

ABOUT THE AUTHOR

Sabina Radeva is a graphic designer and illustrator
based in London, England. In 2008 she graduated
from the Molecular Biology M.Sc. program at
the Max Planck Institute, Germany.
In 2009 she left science for a creative career, and she
has since studied as an illustrator. Sabina is passionate
about projects that blend science with art. She is the
mother of two little girls who are her source of daily
inspiration. Beautifully illustrated, her adaptation of
On the Origin of Species was an immediate sensation
around the world when launched on Kickstarter.

sabinaradeva.com

Blue Fungus Beetle
Gibbifer californicus

Ulysses Butterfly
Papilio ulysses

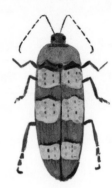

Jewel Beetle
Temognatha spencii

Blue Spot Pansy
Junonia westermanni

Queen Alexandra's Birdwing
Ornithoptera alexandrae

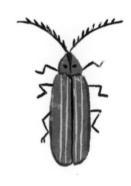

Red-Shouldered Lycid Beetle
Trichalus ampliatus

Yellow Glassy Tiger
Parantica aspasia

Archduke
Lexias satrapes

Goliath Beetle
Goliathus albosignatus

Five-Bar Swordtail
Graphium antiphates

Last's Albatross
Appias lasti

Zigzag Fungus Beetle
Erotylus incomparabilis